THE EGYPTIAN ALCHEMY ORACLE

TIMELESS GUIDANCE FROM ~ THE ANCIENT WORLD ~

STEVE DENHAM

The Egyptian Alchemy Oracle is dedicated to
the truth that being human is to be on a spiritual path.

This edition published in 2025 by Arcturus Publishing Limited
26/27 Bickels Yard, 151–153 Bermondsey Street,
London SE1 3HA

AD012849NT

Card and symbol images courtesy of Steve Denham.
All other images courtesy of Shutterstock.

Printed in China

CONTENTS

FOREWORD

In the famous poem *Portrait of a Lady*, by T S Eliot, the narrative revolves around the liaison between an older woman and a much younger man. At one point, she wistfully observes, 'But our beginnings never know our ends.' The way in which the seeds of *The Egyptian Alchemy Oracle* were planted brings to mind this line, and the truth it expresses so poignantly.

In 2018, while researching a separate writing project, I stumbled across a mysterious little tome – *The Kybalion* – expounding the ancient principles of Hermeticism, otherwise known as mental alchemy or 'mental transmutation'. Sifting through this manifesto, which harks back to the esoteric knowledge of ancient Egypt and purports to articulate the energetic laws that govern the universe, nature and human existence, I realized I had become privy to something quite extraordinary.

Inspired by what I felt to be a body of transcendent knowledge and understanding, I wrote seven 14-line sonnets in honour of these seven age-old nuggets of wisdom, one for each principle. The title, *The Egyptian Alchemy Oracle*, seemed very appropriate, and with that done, I stopped – unsure of what to do at that point or if there was a next step. It lay in the bottom drawer of my desk, until four years later, in 2022 when my wife, Emma Wertheim, and I pursued the world of oracle decks.

While helping Emma realize her vision for Yoga Mudra Oracle (published 2025 by Arcturus), based on yogic hand postures as an adjunct to meditative practice, I realized my sonnets were now called upon by a higher intelligence. With astonishment, before my mind's eye, I witnessed the birth of *The Egyptian Alchemy Oracle*. For each of the seven principles, a 'suit' of seven cards. The blueprint had been cast, with the call to knuckle down to a first draft of this guidebook and, of course, the artistic challenge of creating 49 original paintings, one for every card in the deck.

Special thanks to Emma for her instincts about the look and feel of the cards. Her courage to say why and when a change of direction was needed gave me the belief to start afresh at key points in the process.

We trust and truly hope *The Egyptian Alchemy Oracle* lives up to its name and delivers messages of timeless value for us today.

Steve Denham
Sydney, March 2025

INTRODUCTION

Welcome to *The Egyptian Alchemy Oracle* card deck. At the outset, let's acknowledge *The Kybalion: A Study of The Hermetic Philosophy of Ancient Egypt and Greece*, attributed to the Three Initiates (1908) as the deck's inspirational source. The 49 cards in this divination deck are modern-day expressions of some of the earliest seeds of what author Aldous Huxley named the 'Perennial Philosophy' – humankind's quest through the ages, and many different religions and traditions, to directly experience the divine.

This oracle deck is based on the seven ancient tenets of Hermetic alchemy or Hermeticism, harking back to the Hellenistic period 323-31 BCE, when the revered Hermes Trismegistus (whose surname means 'thrice-great master') reputedly founded the tradition of occult wisdom and was a major contributor to the disciplines of alchemy, astrology, mystic psychology or 'psychic science', theology and philosophy. According to legend, this mysterious figure was an amalgamation of the Greek and Egyptian gods of wisdom, Hermes and Thoth respectively.

In our 21st-century age of information, we are faced with a conundrum. In one sense, everything we need to know is at our fingertips and yet it has never been so easy to lose sight of what's important and what we're really looking for. In the online world we can not only 'get it all' but we can all 'get out there' as we say, with whatever it is we have to offer. This can be seen as the ultimate expression of an egalitarian society. But, at the same time, it has never been so difficult to stand out from the crowd.

Content curation is the trope of our day. We seek what is true and trustworthy in a vast, fathomless sea of information. To quote Samuel Taylor Coleridge's *The Rime of the Ancient Mariner*, 'Water, water, everywhere, Nor any drop to drink.' Of itself, technology is not responsible for overloading our senses. The irony is, to discern right from wrong, true from false, I need a clear and open mind, the eyes to see, and the heart to feel. To seek truth without self-knowledge is to put the cart before the horse.

The seven Hermetic principles reach out to us from antiquity. With their help we open the door to self-mastery encapsulated by the two-word Delphic and Socratic axiom: 'Know thyself.' We embark upon the path that leads to realizing our highest potential. It is an esoteric rule, that the lips of the master come in close when the ears of the student are ready to hear.

Is there reason and purpose behind your coming across *The Egyptian Alchemy Oracle*? The seven principles expressed by the imagery and textual guidance relating to the cards in this deck, are especially unique. Despite being thousands of years old, the truths they convey are not tempered by the social mores of a bygone era. These pristine, inviolable articulations of the human condition, speak to us today with timeless relevance.

Let's open our minds, ears, eyes and hearts to what these expressions of 'inner alchemy' have to offer us. Each principle has a lot to do with energy, but not in the way we normally speak of it. Here we are not talking about electricity, whether that be nuclear, wind turbine or solar-generated. This Oracle deck explores the energy that flows through our inner world, and asks the question, 'Am I destined to be carried along by that energy like a leaf on a running creek or can I learn to be captain of my vessel?'

Every human being is their own power plant. Human energy can be seen as an etheric fingerprint. In this view, the energy each one of us emanates is as characteristic or idiosyncratic to each of us, as are our personalities, attitudes and opinions. Even today there is much to learn about what we mean exactly when we speak of 'my energy' or 'your energy'.

The term is spoken of in everyday life, such as when people say, 'He has boundless energy,' 'I've got no energy today,' or 'My child has too much energy for me.' But this refers to physical vitality or the oomph we need to get out of bed every morning and go about our day. And, of course, we all know about emotions, those fickle fingers with the clout to rule lives and the decisions we make.

As often recognized in the esoteric tradition, it is still only a minority of people who pursue the disciplines required to master one's emotions and lift these energies into a higher chemistry or consciousness. Without effort and understanding, energies are often dissipated in polarizing expressions of fear, love, hate, jealousy, grief, anxiety, and so on.

Ancient traditional alchemy sought to transform base metals into gold. This is a beautiful metaphor for the inner, energetic transformation we seek, guided by these timeless Hermetic tools. With growing understanding and patient practice, we can lift our inner chemistry and being to make the biblical saying 'The kingdom of God is within' our living reality.

The Egyptian Alchemy Oracle is about learning to master the energy of consciousness, understanding how 'lifted chemistry' can transform our lives and allow each one of us to experience 'being' on finer and finer levels. The cards are inspired by what these seven time-honoured principles offer us in today's challenging world: a multifaceted key to realizing our God-given potential.

INTUITED SYMBOLS FOR EACH HERMETIC PRINCIPLE

1. THE ALL IS MIND

The energies of the mind – infinite and finite – are represented by circles within circles and the suggestion of outgoing rays or emanations.

2. CORRESPONDENCE

'As above, so below' – the higher is reflected in the lower, and vice versa. As this symbol emerged, a six-pointed star, the classic motif for this law, magically appeared in the centre.

3. VIBRATION

The perpetual motion of the nanoscopic building blocks of all life, depicted by a progression of circles.

4. POLARITY

The spectrum or continuum expressing the unity of polar opposites across the physical, mental, and spiritual planes.

5. RHYTHM

The cyclic nature of all life – ebb and flow, rise and fall – depicted via wavy, symmetrical lines.

6. CAUSE AND EFFECT

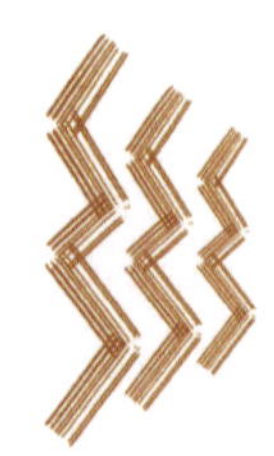

Every effect has a cause, and every cause is, in turn, an effect or result of whatever preceded it. The infinite chain of causation is visually represented by interlocking linear segments.

7. GENDER

The masculine and feminine principles are active in all phenomena – creative, inseparable, dynamic.

HOW DOES THE IMAGERY AND MESSAGING OF THE CARDS RELATE TO EACH PRINCIPLE?

Each principle or suit of seven cards in *The Egyptian Alchemy Oracle* is indicated by the symbol either side of the title on the card. Each suit also has its own 'portal' depicted visually as an archway or entrance.

The colours and elements painted within and around these seven different portals vary, according to the messages conveyed by each card. The archways or portals have symbolic significance. To understand this, first consider the meaning of the imagery on the reverse side of the cards. The crossed keys express the Hermetic notion of 'mental transmutation,' of transforming a base metal – in this case, lead (represented by the lower right-side key cutting) into gold (the lower left-side cutting).

Across the 49 cards, the portals of the seven suits form gateways to backgrounds based on seven themes: nebulae, auroras, the pyramids, waterfalls, oceans, clouds and skies, and sand dunes. These images of earth and

cosmos suggest that a universe of mystery and limitless expansion awaits seekers willing to engage with each principle and turn each of the seven 'keys'.

Thus, the archways are like 'keyholes' or 'doorways' through which hidden worlds and dimensions become accessible.

HOW DO YOU USE EGYPTIAN ALCHEMY ORACLE DECK?

AN INVITATION TO LOVE

Visualizing the seven ancient principles of Hermetic wisdom expressed in modern form was an inspirational moment: an opportunity to blend original poetry and imagery with the magic, artistry, and interpretive guidance of oracle card decks. However, a surprise was in store.

There was a sense of being guided along the way, revisiting the principles in depth, and infusing an ever-unfolding understanding into the themes and aspects that make up the cards in each suit of seven. But there remained the question of how someone might approach the deck as a tool of divination. An unexpected insight arrived.

Where was love? It was mentioned here and there throughout *The Kybalion*'s exposition of the seven great principles, but not on the level you might expect. Love was not presented as a governing law, a fundamental aspect of human nature or for that matter, as an

energetic, universal principle in its own right. It was referred to occasionally – for example, in the discussion of Principle Four (Polarity) love and hate sit at opposite ends of the one emotional continuum. But, as a topic of focus, love seemed to be absent.

At first, this was perplexing. Then, as we say, 'the penny dropped'. Could it be that the user needs to bring their own love to their engagement with *The Egyptian Alchemy Oracle*? Absolutely. Persian poet Rumi said, 'Love is the astrolabe of God's mysteries.' It makes total sense for love to be the key to opening the treasures hidden within the deck. Love is the ingredient, the energy required to purify one's heartfelt seeking and the questions that flow from that. Activate love, and in the process open oneself to what is revealed.

It is vital, therefore, to prepare oneself to engage with *The Egyptian Alchemy Oracle* deck. Over time, as one's understanding grows, our connection with the oracle and its timeless truths, will deepen. But, even from the outset, come to stillness and purity of heart, and, with love at your centre, begin. In this way, each of us who seek direction from *The Egyptian Alchemy Oracle*, embody an 'eighth' key – the transformative energy of love.

PREPARE TO FLY, SOARING ACROSS ALL DIMENSIONS AND BOUNDARIES

The guidebook provides guidance on different card configurations and their meanings. It invites the user's intuitive nature to flourish and forge connections between their soul's purpose on an individual level and the vast, immutable laws that govern nature, human life and the universe.

Every card is like a magic carpet ride, a vehicle to soar across the three great planes of existence – physical, mental and spiritual.

As users we are asked to prepare with attention and intention, to come in touch with higher mind and heart. From there, bring your own 'eighth' key of love to the deck, to activate its tools of divination. In this way, allow its ancient provenance to speak to your heart.

PREPARE – BRING LOVE, THE 'EIGHTH' KEY

Just as matters of the heart can never be formulaic, note that when you seek guidance from *The Egyptian Alchemy Oracle*, there are no fixed rules for how the eighth key of love will help you intuit the number of cards you will pull from the deck on any one occasion, or what configurations you will use.

But to get started, and before you experiment with some suggested (listed below) 'card spread' configurations, try this preparation ritual:

1. Rest the palm of one hand upon the back of the other hand, then with all fingers closed, press your hands to your heart, while sitting still. You can take a meditative posture or whatever feels right for you.

2. Hold this position for as long as you need, aware of your breath, until your attention

moves and flows with the 'in and out' cycle of your breathing.

3. Now direct conscious energy through your hands into your heart, until you feel yourself radiating love – a love that embraces all of life and creation.

4. Close your eyes and hold the deck in both hands. Now gently shuffle the cards. Take your time with this, until it feels right to pull one or more cards.

5. Open your eyes and turn the card, or cards, around to read the title, or titles. Absorb deeply the imagery and symbolism and allow what you see to wash over you.

6. When you are ready to learn more about the card, or the cards you have pulled, open the guidebook, and look up the interpretations for each card, referring to its number within each suit or principle.

SUGGESTED CONFIGURATIONS

Single Key: A single card

Pull just the one card for quick guidance in moments when a decision is needed, with little time to think or analyze.

Crossed Keys: Four-card spread in a 'cross' shape

4. Soul

Spiritual, divine

Earthly, day-to-day

1. Past

2. Future

3. Mind

1. Pull four cards, allowing plenty of time and space between selections.

2. Lay these out with two cards (1, 2) positioned on the horizontal (the earthly, day-to-day dimension), and two cards (3, 4) on the vertical (the spiritual, divine dimension).

3. Understand Card 1 through the lens of your past, and Card 2 your future direction.

4. Understand Card 3 as your mind (habitual thoughts and attitudes) and Card 4 as your pathway to soul expression and destiny.

For the two cards on the horizontal axis, interpret the guidebook readings in the light of your everyday life and questions. For the two cards on the vertical axis, tune in to your spiritual aspirations and quest to grasp your divine purpose.

Master Key: Seven-card spread

Use the Master Key spread when you seek guidance with a major question, enterprise or dilemma. Once you have pulled your seven cards, shuffle these again without turning them around, then lay them out from left to right.

Now turn each card around and read what the guidebook says for each one, carefully noting the principles and themes in the order presented. Try to understand the progression of cards as a movement or 'journey' toward resolving your goal, challenge or project.

Esoterically, seven is the number of the octave, but instead of musical 'notes' think of the cards as 'steps' on the journey you have in mind. Now, think of the transitions from 3 to 4 and 6 to 7 as 'roadblocks', where you will be challenged in some way.

By focusing on the cards and the principles or suits they express in these positions, open yourself intuitively

to what will enable you to move through these transitions or 'rites of passage' to resolve a problem, find an answer or reach your milestone.

INTERPRETING CARD CONFIGURATIONS

Over time, as you repeatedly seek guidance from *The Egyptian Alchemy Oracle*, your own card configurations may reveal themselves to you, in addition to those provided above. Similarly, the way you interpret the guidebook commentary may increasingly become your own – and more applicable to your life, in a quick and transparent way.

You may also sense something magical revealing itself to you as the seeds of new understanding take root and begin to grow and flourish. These ancient principles are interwoven and connected in a way that can only be experienced. Over time, you may realize their boundaries have begun to blur.

Signposts to watch out for

When seeking to understand what the deck is sharing and attempting to communicate to you, look out for the following:

◊ The suit of the card you have chosen, or the weighting of suits among the cards you have selected may highlight the principle/s you need to focus on. For example, if you pull three Polarity cards in the Crossed Keys spread, are you being asked to change direction – physically, mentally or spiritually – by 'polarizing' along one or more continuums of body, mind or spirit? Always take note of which cards fall in the vertical versus the horizontal dimension.

◊ If you repeatedly select cards from one principle, in single or multiple cards pulls, sense deeply what that might mean for your life and soul direction. Are you being asked to change rhythm – Principle Five – in order to open yourself to new learnings and insights? Or are you being made aware that breakthroughs you've already made in areas of your life have come about because, one way or another, there's been a change of vibration (the third principle) or polarity (the fourth)?

◊ If your ambivalence or bewilderment is only amplified through your use of the deck, you are advised to persist. Never be afraid to continue to ask big questions when you consult *The Egyptian*

Alchemy Oracle. It will never cease to reward your tireless pursuit of truth, personal and absolute.

◊ With ongoing use, expect your relationship with the oracle to deepen, especially as your understanding of these ancient principles and their interconnectedness grows. Remember, *The Egyptian Alchemy Oracle* is named in honour of Hermes Trismegistus of Egyptian antiquity, founder of Hermetic Alchemy – a millennia-old body of knowledge able to illuminate the human condition, and even today, offer us timeless credos for transformation.

Open yourself, mind and heart, to the Master Key

Finally, after many consultations and your quest to understand everything *The Egyptian Alchemy Oracle* has to offer, your persistence will be rewarded. Feel the harmony and sense of unity enriching your perception of the world around you. You may find everything is bathed in new meaning, ever deepening and unfolding. Seven becomes one, giving birth to the Master Key.

REVERSE SIDE OF THE CARDS

SYMBOLISM

The image on the back of the cards is a collage of depth and meaning. The silhouette of a keyhole represents what *The Egyptian Alchemy Oracle* offers its reader – a doorway or portal to new understandings, new vision, new being.

Around the keyhole is etched the ancient symbol of alchemy, best known as the Philosopher's Stone, representing a mystical substance capable of turning base metals into precious metals such as gold or silver. The same symbolism expands to embrace the quest to realize one's divine potential.

As the overarching symbol or Master Key for *The Egyptian Alchemy Oracle*, the illuminated crossed keys represent Hermetic alchemy, or 'mental transmutation'. The ends of each key are significant – the lower left tip and 'cutting', as this shape is described by locksmiths, is the alchemical symbol of the sun or gold. The lower right cutting is the alchemical symbol for lead, a base metal. Together, for this oracle deck, the two keys represent the esoteric, inner process of enlightenment each of us aspire to – in the sense of 'transforming lead into gold'.

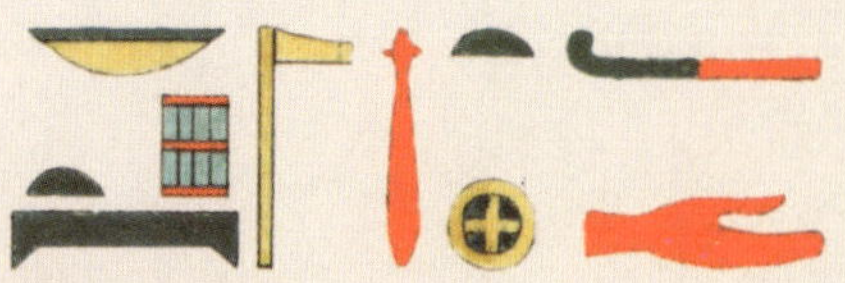

THE ALL IS MIND

I

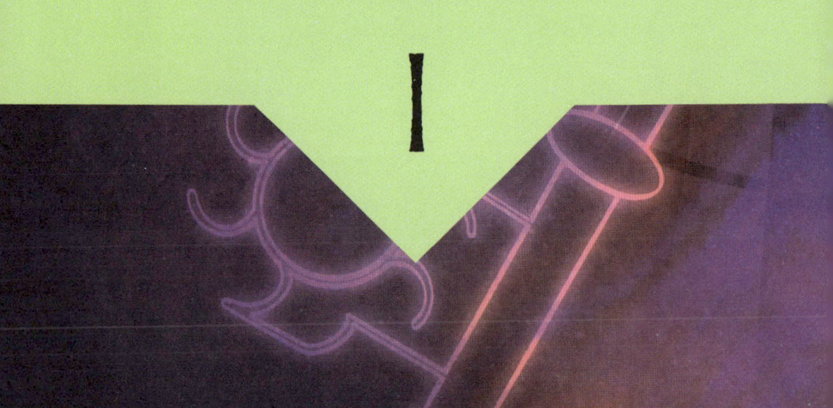

The world is within
Like running sap inside bark.
Tree's mind, mind is tree.

The Hermetic alchemists have 'gold' to share with us. And what they have to say can take you by surprise. *The Egyptian Alchemy Oracle* is an invitation to open our minds to an ancient body of knowledge, as relevant to the human condition today as it was thousands of years ago. It calls us to step outside of self-imposed limitations, to realize a potential that goes beyond anything we may have thought or imagined.

The first of the seven Hermetic axioms declares, 'THE ALL is Mind': the universe is mental, it exists in the 'mind of THE ALL'. Of course, we all know 'mind' is important. It sets us apart from the rest of nature. In the world we live in, the human mind occupies a special position. It is a marvel of 'engineering', a miracle of creation. However, the Hermetists take all this a step further.

The first principle declares that *everything* is mental – that all life, creation and the universe, including humanity, are held in 'higher mind' or 'infinite living mind'. This goes way beyond our ordinary understanding of what we mean when we speak of 'mind' – mine, yours or ours. And even though it may feel natural to speak of 'God', remember Hermeticism is not a religion or 'religious'.

If we are prepared to at least entertain the idea that everything is mental in nature, we gain a fragment of insight into the esoteric alchemist's art of 'mental transmutation'. At the highest level, this was said to be capable of changing the conditions of the universe, including matter and the elements.

The importance of mind – including our thoughts, attitudes and opinions – is widely recognized today in mainstream life. Clearly, however, this first Hermetic principle, sometimes referred to as mentalism, exalts the influence and potential of the mind and mental energy to a higher power.

This is not to suggest mental development at this level is common. In fact, *The Kybalion* claims only history's most advanced mental alchemists – meaning very few individuals – have developed the ability to control physical phenomena including storms, earthquakes, winds and the like.

For the moment, *The Egyptian Alchemy Oracle* asks us to simply entertain the possibility that such examples of humankind have existed and may exist today. As a starting point, it is easy to see that hierarchies exist in life and throughout creation on our planet – from the humble earthworm to more advanced animals, and on to human beings with the potential for higher consciousness. Bear in mind, too, that what any person can perceive or experience at any given moment, relies to some extent on their own thought processes and state of mind.

The wisdom of the Hermetists inspires us forward. With the will to evolve and the willingness to learn how to use the 'tools' at our disposal, human beings have the potential to rise in the hierarchy of creation. The greater our understanding of the timeless laws that govern the great physical, mental and spiritual planes, the more we can act in harmony with those principles, ascend the scale of being and attract experiences of soul in higher dimensions.

The principle of mentalism, 'The ALL is Mind', is the foundation of the Hermetic teaching. It represents mental transmutation – the same process which allows us to grasp all seven axioms and bring them to life in a creative way. It is the key of keys.

OPEN YOUR MIND

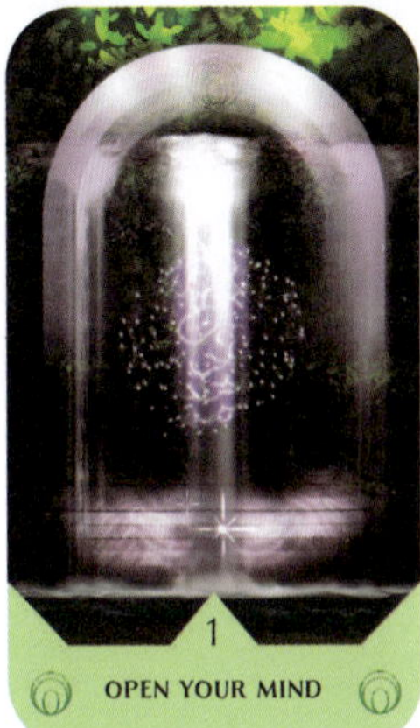

Let go of everything you believe or ever thought you knew.

~

What is real or not real? What is true or not true? And have you ever wondered who is asking?

The first great Hermetic principle, THE ALL is Mind, raises the question of how a finite human being can comprehend infinite mind. It is an expression of the Divine Paradox.

To the creator, the universe is said to be like a dream or state of meditation, while to finite human beings, the world must be regarded as real. Our life, actions and thoughts are all based on what we assume to be 'reality'. But in the words of Shakespeare's *Hamlet*, 'There's the rub.' For just as we are contained within THE ALL, so each of us must represent the creator – meaning THE ALL is also within each of us.

The Open Your Mind card is an opportunity to start again with a fresh outlook on everything you ever thought or believed to be true about your life, or a situation you may find yourself in right now.

The first card in the suit calls you to walk the path of mental transmutation. A new way of thinking allows you let go of old ways, thoughts and attitudes and embark on the path of spiritual growth.

By grasping the unity that resolves paradox and contradiction, you can fuse polar opposites into true wisdom. Prepare yourself to drink deeply of the Hermetic teaching and invite the transforming power of its seven ancient principles into your life and being.

2 PURIFY YOUR ATTENTION

Release distraction, reclaim attention.

Do you find yourself constantly switching from one thing to another? Are you in a continuous state of distraction?

The first great Hermetic principle highlights the crisis of attention in the 21st century. A tsunami of information competes daily for our mental focus across multiple virtual platforms – social media, text, email, podcasts – in business, advertising, and marketing.

As artificial intelligence becomes more sophisticated and invasive, we need to find a way to claim back our capacity for deep thinking and sustained focus.

The Purify Your Attention card urges you to heed the call of the ancients, to see and grasp what is happening today and take every step to come back to your authentic, creative self. Meditation, the conscious breath, stillness – the tools you need are at your disposal.

You hold the wisdom of the eternal within you. By understanding and putting into practical application this and all the great Hermetic principles, you learn to purify and reclaim your 'attention', the innate power of your mind to reflect the cosmos in thought, imagination and vision.

ATTRACT YOUR LIFE

Your mind is a cosmic jewel, your innate gateway to rebirth and higher consciousness.

~

Do you feel the need to break the momentum of your life and its current demands? Do you seek new directions in your career, home life or relationships?

It's no accident you've pulled the Attract Your Life card. You're at the top of the steps, guided by angelic beings. The doorway is open, summon the courage and the faith to step forward into the unknown.

The third card in THE ALL is Mind suit reminds you of a great truth. What you believe becomes your life. Your mind – its thoughts, imagination, hopes and beliefs – is the key to realizing your destiny, higher purpose, and fulfilling your divine potential.

Everything you have experienced up to now, good and bad, has been necessary. Allow for this with love. It has prepared you for this moment.

You've already attracted the support and everything you've needed to reach this point. All you need to do is keep going! You are called to truly grasp and understand this law, and step through the portal.

4 TO RECEIVE, LET GO

Create the space to receive new purpose, new being.

How is it possible to think and feel in a different way? Do you seek new life and being, but you're not sure where to start?

The first great Hermetic principle expresses the truth that just as 'THE ALL is Mind' and the 'universe is mental', so our life, being and destiny are products of the human mind – our capacity to focus, think, understand, imagine, project and make manifest.

We can be oblivious to the creative power of the human mind in the non-stop train of thoughts and associations in our daily life. To take the path less travelled, first become aware of the automatic, mechanical quality of our thinking.

The fourth card in the suit, 'To receive, let go', reminds us of one of the great esoteric laws, that to be truly present to our lives and become the best version of ourselves, we need to move beyond the need to own or possess.

To allow your true self to step free, this card calls you to let go of everything that consumes you – precious objects and possessions, your pet loves or hates, strong emotions or opinions. Consciously release them all.

Embark upon the path of spiritual growth and realize your soul potential. Consciousness is the light of the mind that reveals all. Turn it on and live, wholly and truly.

EMBRACE THE LIGHT UNKNOWN

In the midst of the unknown, new understanding is born.

~

Why is 'not knowing' important? Can you let go of the need to be 'in the know'?

The first great Hermetic principle declares that the infinite mind of the All is the 'womb of universes'. Don't worry if you find this hard to understand. The Hermetists add: 'In its essence, THE ALL is unknowable.'

The gift of consciousness helps us to extrapolate from 'finite mind', to begin to appreciate what the Hermetic teaching describes as 'infinite, living mind'.

You are invited to take the plunge into the unknown, to bathe in contemplation of the eternal. Allow yourself to be both confronted and guided by the Divine Paradox of the Hermetic teaching: that all life and creation, including humankind, exists entirely within the 'meditative, dream state' of the infinite mind of the All, and yet we must base our life, actions and thoughts on its concrete reality.

The fifth card in THE ALL is Mind suit, 'Embrace the light unknown', urges you to heed the call of the Hermetic teachers to 'Keep your mind ever on the star, but let your eyes watch over your footsteps, lest you fall into the mire by reason of your upward gaze.'

You are called to surrender to the great mystery of the universe and human existence. Let go of your knowing and your need to know. Step upon the path that leads to the light.

6 FOCUS YOUR MIND

Transformation is a state of mind.

Do you need to let go of fixed ideas and old opinions? Are you ready to look at your life and your purpose in a new light? Is there another way?

The first great Hermetic principle challenges our ordinary thinking. If the world is mental, how can our feet literally find solid ground? Are rocks and trees, buildings and other humans not real? Does this 'truth' reduce everything to ethereal, inner imagery?

As they often do, the Hermetic teachers claim the answer is both 'yes' and 'no'. If you think about it, we can't know the external world outside of our sensory perceptions related to everything and everyone around us.

Remember that famous question, 'If a tree falls in the forest and no one is around to hear it, does it make a sound?' Without getting lost in philosophical speculation, the idea that we acquire knowledge through our senses is a useful starting point for grasping the importance of mind in relation to how you advance along the path of spiritual evolution.

The sixth card in THE ALL is Mind suit, 'Focus your mind', calls you to deepen your understanding of this first great principle. THE ALL is Mind – the universe, your quality of life, and your level of being all rely on your ability to focus your mind. In the simplest terms, you need to focus to put into daily practice the tools of physical, mental and spiritual transformation.

SIMPLY BELIEVE

Whatever you believe becomes your truth.

Do you believe in yourself? If what you believe becomes your truth, how does that affect your life?

The first great Hermetic principle – 'THE ALL is Mind; the universe is mental' – aligns with 'truths' recognized in business and professional life: in politics, sport, religion and faith. Completing any task at hand involves focus, attention and commitment, including the determination to never give up, to overcome challenges, and emerge successful.

There is no shortage of examples throughout history that exemplify the power of the mind, in service of either the good or the bad. Remarkable stories of courage and the will to overcome all obstacles are well known to us, as well as, unfortunately, dark chapters and periods when dictators or ruthless leaders used their mental powers to abuse their authority.

The seventh card in THE ALL is Mind suit, 'Simply believe', urges you to understand the relationship of 'belief' to mind and being. The simple, unshakeable confidence in your own abilities or commitment to a methodology, philosophy or faith, can conquer all obstacles and transform your life and yourself – heart, mind and soul.

Whatever you believe becomes your truth, your reality. What you believe about yourself, becomes who you are.

CORRESPONDENCE

II

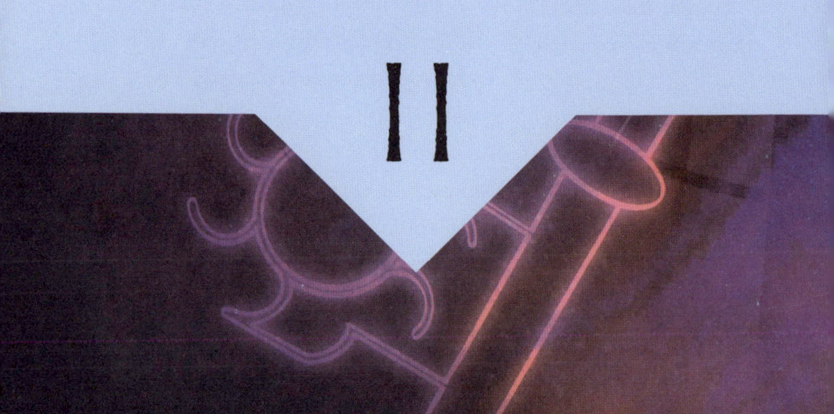

The distant is near
As your toes sift
through the earth
To enfold the stars.

The Hermetic principle of 'Correspondence' is also known as 'As above, so below', symbolized by the six-pointed star that is formed by two overlapping triangles, one pointing up, the other down. By understanding the 'lower', we gain insight into the nature of what is 'higher'. Everything is relative.

The universe, our planet and all manifestations of life – mineral, plant, animal, human and divine – are all part of a vast continuum of being, from the lowest vibration of the physical plane, rising upward to the mental sphere, and on to the highest vibration of the spiritual plane.

The second principle draws our attention to the order and symmetry of creation, and of humanity's place within the universe. We are beings with the potential to ascend or descend, both within each plane, or from one plane to another, the physical to the mental, and ever upwards to the spiritual. As a tool of thought, it helps us to understand the energetic nature of our world and open our senses to new worlds of experience.

The 13th-century Persian poet Rumi said, 'Love is the astrolabe of God's mysteries', applying the metaphor of an ancient instrument for calculating the altitude of celestial bodies, to convey the power of love to penetrate the higher planes of existence. Think of Sir Isaac Newton and his discovery of gravity, which applies as much to distant planets as earthbound bodies and objects.

Correspondence gives us a way of approaching things that we may otherwise just think of as 'unknown'. It helps us ask questions that already plant the seeds of an answer. For instance, does the relationship between the mental and the physical – a well-worn pathway of investigation – allow us to speculate about how the spiritual might relate to the mental?

Theories about the unconscious showed how repressed emotions and thoughts could be expressed or made manifest through conscious language and the symptoms of the physical body. The interplay between spiritual aspirations and our mental world is similar.

Guided by the principle of correspondence, we direct our attention to how the great physical, mental and spiritual planes reflect and shed light on each other. For example, grasping the laws that govern the human body gives us a starting point for investigating the origin and meaning of our thoughts and emotional life. Similarly, everything we have learned about our mental and emotional world helps us approach the spiritual realm.

'As above, so below' reminds us of the profound interconnectedness of life across all dimensions. The lower illuminates the higher and, in turn, by opening ourselves to the divine, our knowledge of the lower expands.

Just as the world and the universe are in a constant state of motion and evolution, so, as members of humanity, we have a boundless potential to evolve as multi-dimensional beings.

FROM THE LOWER, GLIMPSE THE HIGHER

1

Asking big questions with all your heart, brings closer everything you are seeking.

~

Do you have a deep sense there must be more? Do you expect to have to make huge sacrifices, or travel to distant places to find what you are looking for?

Your path ahead is being illuminated. All will become clear. Your deeply felt intuition that there must be more is nudging you in the right direction. Simply believe.

The first card in this suit, 'From the lower, glimpse the higher', calls you to step through this portal of light. Let go of all fear. Remember, this principle – Correspondence – is also known as 'As above, so below'. Anything you already can do, or know well, is of value on the higher planes.

The moon above the waters, representing your inner life – feelings, aspirations, desires, emotions – is bathed in starry light from the heavens.

Your journey is within. There is nowhere else you need to be. Here, you are loved in a way that goes beyond anything you've ever experienced. The worlds converge to support you on your path – heart and soul, earth and heaven.

2 FEEL THE UNIVERSE YOU ARE

To explore the universe, look inside yourself.

~

Where are you looking for answers to life's deepest questions? And who is looking?

No matter how small we may be or feel, we are all part of, and connected to, the infinite. In our own unique way, each of us is a universe within, reflecting the boundlessness around us and reminding us of our own limitless potential.

The English poet William Blake poignantly expressed this age-old truth with the words:

To see a world in a grain of sand
And heaven in a wildflower
Hold infinity in the palm of your hand
And eternity in an hour.

'As above, so below; as below, so above,' say our Hermetic forefathers. This miraculous symmetry is manifested at every level of life and creation, within and between each of the great physical, mental and spiritual planes of existence.

The second card in Correspondence suit, 'Feel the universe you are,' calls on you to open heart, mind and soul to your God-given potential and birthright.

Everything you need, you already have; the seed of the divine is planted within you – you were born with it. You are indeed that grain containing a world of possibility.

INVITE SPIRIT IN

Be liberated by the mystery of spirit.

What do we really know? Even if you don't have all the answers, do you realize how miraculous you are?

'As within, so without' and 'As above, so below' – across all planes and dimensions of existence. Every bit of knowledge and experience we possess helps to illuminate the mystery.

Just as we know very little about gravity, other than describing it as 'the force that pulls two masses toward each other', so we may struggle to understand emotions, feelings, thoughts, even though we have names for those too – love/hate, joy/despair, courage/fear, and so on.

On the spiritual plane, we experience a whole new dimension of the unknown. Spirit is pure mystery. Yet, like the forces we know in physics, its effects are visible and known. In The Gospel of John, we read, 'The wind blows where it wishes, and you hear its sound, but you do not know where it comes from or where it is going.'

The third card in this suit, 'Invite spirit in', calls you to be vulnerable, to drop your guard and let go of the need to know. In this space, you allow for spirit to work its magic.

Angelic beings and forces are on your side, supporting your growth and evolution for the good of all humankind. Gather up the faith of your heart and lift its vibration toward the light.

EXPAND YOUR BEING

Release, step free and open, allow for expansion.

~

Are you listening to your heart? Can you really only trust your thinking?

Fresh air blows through conventional thoughts and opinions about what is real or not real, true or false. The inspiration comes to drop fixed or narrow attitudes about finer worlds and higher beings.

'As above, so below' reminds us that 'that which seeks' is an unavoidable component of our quest for knowledge. Even the science of physics acknowledges that what is observed is altered by the observer.

Open yourself to new levels of being and soul development. No learning or experience is wasted. Everything you already know and have experienced is a stepping stone toward ever-evolving truth.

The fourth card in the Correspondence suit, 'Expand your being', calls you to tune in your awareness of life and creation on the higher planes of existence. By penetrating the essence of what lies below, you break through the veils that separate you from what waits for you above.

Remember the words of the Hermetists, 'When the ears of the seeker are open, the lips of wisdom come in close.'

BECOME A CREATOR

The seeds of the divine lie within us.

Have you ever thought of yourself as a child of God? What would happen if you nurtured the seeds of your divine potential?

'As above, so below' is an ancient law that applies in many different ways. For example, the biblical book of *Genesis* says, 'So God created mankind in his image, in the image of God he created them; male and female he created them.'

A captain of a ship may speak of their cruise liner as a 'she'; we talk about the weather being 'miserable', the sun 'smiling down' or about the influence of 'Lady Luck'. And we regard our pet dogs and cats as members of our families, who understand every word we say and know what support to provide us, when we need it.

In a similar way, our Hermetic forefathers attribute 'mind, soul and life' to the mineral kingdom. They say that even molecules, atoms and corpuscles have their 'loves' and 'hates'; 'likes' and 'dislikes'; 'attractions' and 'repulsions'.

The fifth card in this suit, 'Become a creator', reminds you that you are far more than a just a cog in the wheel of life on this planet. It is your time. You are called to take action, to claim your divine birthright and become a creator in your own right.

6 DISCOVER YOUR ANSWER WITHIN

The answers to your deepest questions lie within.

Have you ever thought of yourself as possessing divine blessings? What would happen if you accepted that?

The second great Hermetic principle, 'As above, so below', bathes the world around us in new light. We observe the hierarchical nature of all life and creation, across all kingdoms – mineral, animal and human.

Even if we are sceptical about the existence of angels, archangels and demigods, we can still grasp that, if they are real and not mythical, they must surely exist in another dimension. The Hermetists call this the spiritual plane.

Think of it this way, 'As within, so without'. The 'I am' that is each of us is contained within the greater, 'I am that I am' of the biblical book of Exodus.

The sixth card in the Correspondence suit, 'Discover your answer within', calls you to see and know that, even as you are, you are perfect and complete. And so everything you seek, and the guidance you wish with all your heart to receive, lies within, waiting for the kiss that will rouse it from unconsciousness.

Open yourself, heart and mind. See with new eyes, hear with new ears. You have been given so much. Everything you are looking for, you already have.

OPEN TO YOUR COSMIC DESTINY

Your higher purpose is awaiting your discovery and realization.

~

What is it you are meant to do? What would it mean for you to follow your divine path?

The second great Hermetic maxim sheds new light on every aspect of who you are and everything you may have ever thought to be true about your chosen life path.

'What do you do?' The question is familiar. We all make a living through whatever opportunities come our way. And sometimes we may feel like where and how we end up putting our skills and knowledge to practical use is determined by no more than chance.

'Fate', 'fortune', 'providence', 'karma' or 'predestination' are words we often hear when speaking of destiny and what this might mean individually for each of us.

The seventh card in this suit calls you to tune in to where life is calling you, to follow the stirrings of your gut, heart and soul.

Your highest destiny is about much more than your choice of what you do for a job, or the love of your life. You are asked to surrender to higher will and guidance; to take your next step in faith and follow your intuitive compass.

Know you are part of a bigger picture. No matter how tough things may be at times, or what regrets you have, you are being bathed in everlasting love. You are on track. Believe. Your cosmic destiny beckons.

VIBRATION

III

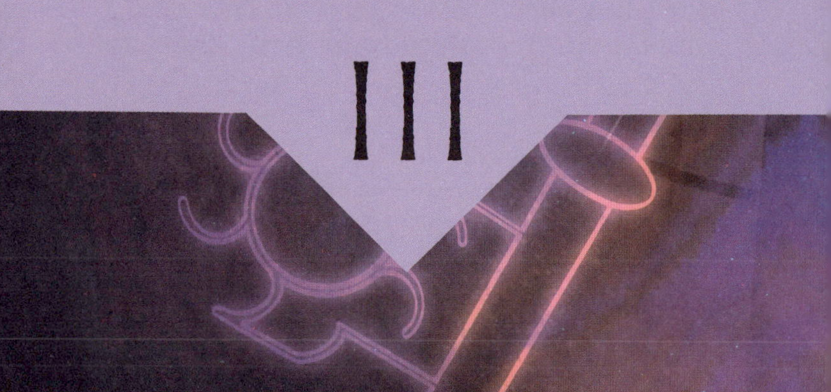

Stillness is nowhere
The inward mountain quivers
Ever unceasing ascend.

The third Hermetic principle, Vibration, aligns with the famous saying of ancient Greek philosopher Heraclitus: 'No man ever steps in the same river twice.' Everything in the universe is in flux, a state of impermanence.

Nothing is still. We may imagine things around us, including ourselves, to be solid, stable and able to come to a physical stop or motionless state. But at the micro level, objects are composed of vibrating molecules, even if our senses are not capable of perceiving that motion.

The third principle tells us all matter and forms of energy are 'modes of vibratory motion'. The science of atomic and sub-atomic particles, quantum mechanics, verifies that all of creation is constantly changing and moving. Hard or dense physical matter like bricks or rocks or gemstones are composed of nanoscopic particles – protons, neutrons and electrons – in a constant state of motion or vibration.

And this is just the beginning, when we consider the three great planes of existence – physical, mental, spiritual. Exploring the invisible nature of our world, we come across finer energies in the higher subdivisions of the physical plane. These are well-known aspects of our everyday life, including heat, light, magnetism, electricity, gravity and other forms of attraction.

When we reach the mental plane, we encounter phenomena often characterized as speculative or 'pseudo-science', including accounts of psychic phenomena, mysticism and the occult. However, by understanding the relationship between lower and higher planes and their subdivisions, in a way that aligns even a little bit with our life journey, we may entertain the possibility of higher planes of existence – even if, so far we may have no direct experience of them.

The Hermetists advise us the degree or rate of vibration distinguishes planes of existence and their subdivisions from each other. Further, they say that in addition to length, breadth and height, vibration is a fourth measurable 'dimension' of everything that exists. From phenomena we are familiar with on lower levels to the higher levels we may know little about, it all comes down to vibration.

The principle of Vibration offers an invaluable insight: that the 'rate of vibration' determines where everything and anything, including ourselves, sit on the scale of being. In this way, the Hermetists show us that sub-atomic particles, the human mind and the being of an archangel are all fundamentally the same, differentiated only by vibratory degree or frequency.

Similar to the nature of established manifestations of energy – heat, light, electricity and magnetism – we may now consider the possibility that our will, thoughts, emotions, reasonings and desires are also forms of vibratory motion.

With the master key of 'mental transmutation', the Hermetists guide us through the portal that opens to a whole new dimension of life. We all have the potential to consciously increase the rate of vibration of our mental states, positively influencing others and the world around us, lifting our 'chemistry', and opening ourselves to experiences on the spiritual plane.

LIFT YOUR CHEMISTRY

Higher purpose is awaiting your discovery and realization.

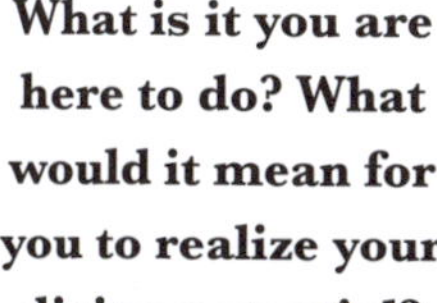

What is it you are here to do? What would it mean for you to realize your divine potential?

The third ancient Hermetic principle, Vibration, helps you tune in to the 'chemistry' of your being, and consciously raise its vibration. Even just believing we can gain some control in this respect is a step towards learning to refine your physical, mental and spiritual being – and experience life at higher and higher planes and frequencies.

There is more to 'chemistry' than meets the eye. It is a well-known subject of study at school or university, conjuring up classroom images of bubbles and beakers. But chemistry can also be understood in the sense of the quality of energy each of us manifests in the world at any given moment, whether that be coarse or fine, intense or relaxed, earthy or ethereal, restless or calm, caring or careless.

The 'Lift your chemistry' card is calling you to be responsible for the energy you 'put out' or emanate, even though there may be very little understanding of this in everyday life. By learning to raise the vibration of your being, you become more in touch with the higher aspect of yourself and move forward on the path of fulfilling your true destiny and soul potential.

2 MOVE INTO FLOW

Harmonize with the vibration of all life and creation.

~

Do you know that everything is in motion? What is the value of flow?

The third great Hermetic principle tells us everything is in motion. This is easily verified when we observe clouds, gases, water, fire or the action of wind. Animal and plant life, too, are constantly and visibly moving.

But this is also true of objects of substantial weight and mass – stones, minerals, rocks, and land formations – or man-made structures such as apartment blocks, roads, and bridges.

Modern science confirms that everything in our world, both living and inanimate, is composed of atoms. Each atom consists of a nucleus containing positively charged protons and neutral neutrons, around which negatively charged electrons are in orbit. The forces that hold atoms together are primarily electromagnetic in nature, with the attraction between the positively charged protons and negatively charged electrons creating atomic stability. The vibratory force of attraction between protons and electrons creates atomic stability. It is the 'glue' of all creation.

'Move into flow' calls you to align your being with the cycles, forces and energies of the universe. By becoming aware of your own personal vibration, you attune yourself to a special inner kind of motion. In the state and experience of flow, access your creative nature. Let go of resistance, bring yourself into harmony.

COME TO STILLNESS 3

In the midst of unceasing motion and activity – stop.

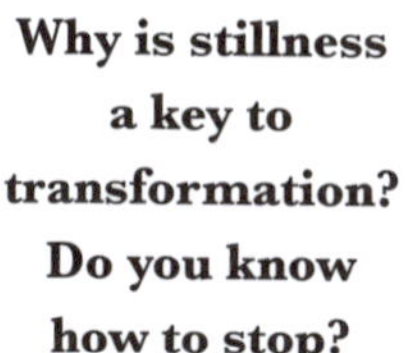

Why is stillness a key to transformation? Do you know how to stop?

The third great ancient Hermetic principle calls us to consciously bring our mind/body continuum to a state of stillness. The importance of being still is universally recognized as being beneficial – sleep, rest and having 'time out' are some of the fundamental methods by which we can change our level of vibration.

However, stillness also relates to our spiritual life. The Bible (Psalm 46:10) says, 'Be still, and know that I am God.' Similarly, Indian spiritual master Meher Baba famously said, 'Mind working is man, mind working fast is mad, mind slowed down is *mast* (holy), mind stopped is God.' In this quote, 'mast' is from the Sufi term 'mast-Allah' meaning 'intoxicated with God'.

There are many ways to quieten one's mind. In our 21st-century age of information, finding a technique or practice to achieve this is only a Google search away. However, whatever approach you are attracted to, persistence is required. Without focus, today's instant accessibility to everything known can end up distracting us from realizing our soul potential.'Come to stillness' reminds you that experience is the litmus test of truth. Embrace the transforming quality of stillness. Discover the finer vibratory aspect of being, and step through the portal to experience your higher self and the world of spirit.

4 SHOOT FOR THE STARS

Lift your being, your 'I am' and reach toward the heavens.

Are you aware of your limitless potential? Do you truly know yourself?

'All is metaphoric of the mystery.' A common thread unites human beings and subatomic particles, connecting even a single-celled organism in biology, known as the 'monad', with the being of an 'archangel'.

Everything is subject to the third great Hermetic principle of Vibration. The difference is just a matter of degree. Grasping this is a vital key to understanding the nature of all life on this planet and our human potential for transformation.

Everything vibrates – on all levels and planes of being. Consciousness, the capacity of a human being to 'know thyself', as we recall from the ancient Greek oracle at Delphi, is our greatest gift; it is the seed of the divine within us all.

The fourth card in the Vibration suit, 'Shoot for the stars', calls you back to your sacred birthright, to take the path of spiritual transformation leading to the stars. It is never too late.

Become aware of the quality of energy you are manifesting. Take a conscious breath and raise the vibration of your mantra 'I am' onwards and ever upward.

TRANSCEND THE LAWS 5

Lift your rate of vibration, rise above laws and limitations that no longer serve you.

Can you recall moments of clarity in your life? Times when you sensed your mind and body working together in a way that felt weightless and harmonious. Would you like to repeat this experience?

Experience is the wellspring of life, the foundation of your being. Give and you will receive. However, sometimes it is simply given to you, as a gift – even if you don't know why.

The fifth card in the suit of Vibration, 'Transcend the laws', brings you the key to many questions. Know that vibration underlies all life, creation and the universe. For humanity, it is a measure of mind, body and soul.

You stand at the threshold. Vibration puts the key to transformation in your hands. To step through the portal, look no further than your own ability to raise your level of vibration.

Through meditation and the conscious breath, lift the 'chemistry' of your thinking and feeling nature. With wings of lifted vibration, take flight beyond old laws and restrictions.

Move ever up the scale of being, from the physical to the mental, and ever higher, to experience the spiritual plane and its learnings. In deepening love, ascend toward the light.

6 BOW TO THE MIRACULOUS

In humility, surrender to the great mystery

~

Do you realize you, your being and your life are miraculous? What if it's only your thinking that stands in your way?

Open to the miraculous. There are things we have the capacity to do, which are within our reach, that we may have thought impossible.

Whether they are fact or myth, the miracles attributed to prophets and holy teachers still convey great wisdom and truth.

The Hermetists tell us that highly evolved examples of humanity throughout history have understood the laws and forces that govern the physical, mental, and spiritual worlds and have been able to master these at will.

Shakespeare's Hamlet says, 'There are more things in Heaven and Earth, Horatio, than are dreamt of in your philosophy.' Perhaps it is not stretching one's imagination too far to believe that advanced souls have walked, and continue to walk, among us, even if they go unrecognized.

The sixth card in this suit, 'Bow to the miraculous', reminds you that raising your vibration will carry you across the threshold of new worlds and dimensions, allowing you to touch upon your true self and destiny.

In higher truth and vibratory motion, open yourself to transformation and the realization of your divine potential. Become the miracle you seek.

BE THE TRANSFORMER 7

Your birthright is to become a vessel of light.

Do you know you are pure vibration? Have you ever explored your innate ability to lift the vibration of your body, thoughts and emotions?

The third great Hermetic principle is one of the great keys to self-mastery. It reminds us we are powerful beings with the innate capacity to raise and refine our level of vibration and evolve in the hierarchy of creation.

We are travellers in a cosmic world, surrounded by miraculous phenomena – heat, light, colour, magnetism, electricity, radio waves, gravitation – the existence of which is indisputable, and deployed by the human-made technologies essential to our everyday life.

The seventh card in the suit of Vibration, 'Be the transformer', calls you to look within, to see that you, too, are a transcendent being; that the gift of consciousness is God-given, and yours to use at will.

Harnessing your vibratory energy, shine a light into the depths of darkness and illuminate the pathway to the heavens.

As one exponent of the great Hermetic teaching described it: 'He who understands the principle of Vibration has grasped the sceptre of power.'

POLARITY

IV

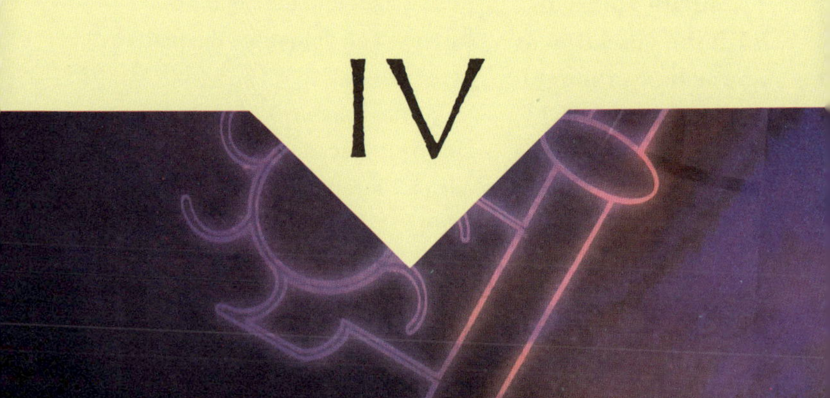

Opposites are one
It’s a matter of degree
Transcend toward sun.

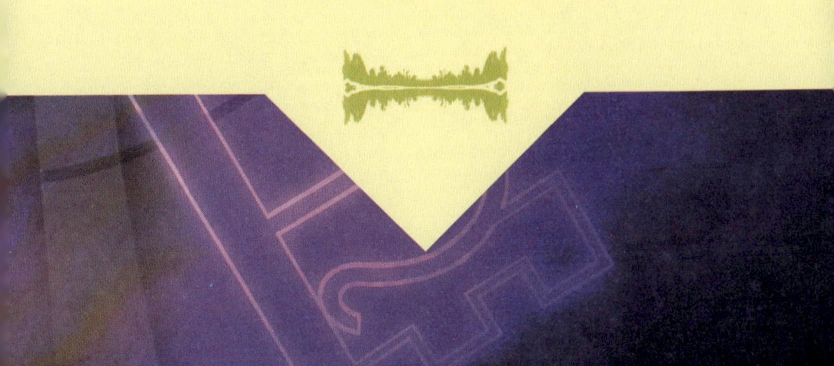

Exploring the fourth great Hermetic principle of Polarity, we begin to grasp the interconnectedness of these great axioms and how they work together to bring about 'mental transmutation'.

The fourth principle recognizes the dual nature of everything, all forms of life and creation: two extremes or opposites are contained within the one, creating a whole. We see that different degrees of vibratory motion, as explored in the third principle, characterize the continuum between the opposing poles of an object, entity or manifestation.

Is it possible the great Italian polymath Leonardo da Vinci was alluding to the esoteric meaning of polarity when he said, 'Among the great things which are to be found among us, the being of nothingness is the greatest'? Perhaps he was suggesting that this is the origin or womb from which everything is born; that nothingness and existence sit at opposite ends of the great continuum of life.

On the physical plane, night and day represent different degrees of light, a spectrum ranging from the absence of light to its full presence. In the visible spectrum, light exists as a range of frequencies that we perceive as different colours, from the lowest to highest frequency: red, orange, yellow, green, blue, indigo and violet. At the highest level, all these frequencies combine to create white light, which contains the full spectrum.

In the same way, temperature measures the vibrational energy of atoms, molecules and ions that make up matter. As the rate of vibratory motion decreases, matter moves from hot to warm, to cool, and finally to cold. Conversely, increasing the vibratory motion of particles raises the temperature, moving from cold to hot.

The fourth principle proposes that all material and natural manifestations in our world represent a unity of opposites; being different degrees of the same thing, whether that be temperature, light or colour.

When we investigate the mental plane, this axiom comes to life in a startling way, leaving no doubt as to why it is a 'key' within the Hermetic system. We reflect on continuums that involve aspects of our emotional and intellectual life – for example, melancholy/joy, courage/fear or love/hate. Obviously, experiences on either side of these dichotomies are very different but understanding how these opposing poles represent different degrees of the same 'stuff' opens the door to mental transmutation. We are intrigued by the possibility of consciously shifting our inner states from one pole to the other.

Finally, on the mental and spiritual planes, we may have experienced the changing of our own states, shepherded toward the 'light' by the higher vibration of another person, teacher or mentor. This is a gift. It is proof of what is possible for us. It inspires us to 'polarize' ourselves but also demonstrates, beyond doubt, we can help others and, even more, we can raise the chemistry of all life and creation on this planet.

POLARIZE UP ON YOUR BOOTSTRAPS

1

Lift your being, evolve toward spirit.

Can you imagine yourself as a soul being? Are you ready to make extraordinary efforts?

Like a winged messenger sent from above, what the fourth great Hermetic principle has to say to us is clear and liberating. Think 'polarize', shift your consciousness toward the light.

Polarity relates to the idea of two poles that sit at either end of a continuum. In everyday life, we are familiar with hot/cold, wet/dry, hard/soft, and so on. In the mental world, this applies to our emotions, feelings, thoughts and attitudes, such as hate/love, pessimism/optimism, fear/courage and pain/pleasure.

The world of spirit is at one end of the spectrum of all life and creation, with the opposite pole composed of the lowest forms of matter. Human beings are like seeds planted by a higher intelligence. Having taken root in soil, a seedling grows instinctively toward the sun. It is the same with our divine nature.

The first card in the suit of Polarity, 'Polarize up on your bootstraps', calls you to 'polarize' your being toward higher and higher planes, moving from the physical to the mental to the spiritual. It's the spiritual equivalent of 'pulling yourself up by your bootstraps'. Transformation begins with understanding and learning to use the 'tools' that are available to you to achieve this. Focus, understand, and act. Believe you can, and you will.

2 EXIST FINITE, RISE ETERNAL

Change is constant and opposites are one.

Are you confused by life's contradictions? Do you seek definite answers but end up perplexed?

The fourth great Hermetic principle reminds us that truth is not black and white. The human condition is not a riddle that can be solved like a mathematical equation – it is a reality to be experienced. Life is both divided and unified.

The Greek philosopher Heraclitus said life is always in flux. As we've seen, his famous declaration was: 'No man ever steps into the same river twice.' On the one hand, it is the same river and the same man, but it is equally true that both have changed.

As finite beings, we humans have a beginning and an end – birth and death. And yet each of us carries the seed of the divine. We are both finite and infinite.

The second card in the suit of Polarity, 'Exist finite, rise eternal', invites you to understand that 'polarizing' can be a conscious act. Polarize your thoughts, emotions, and attitudes towards the light. From the lower end, lift toward the higher.

Self-mastery on the mental plane opens the door to the spiritual. Matter and spirit are polar opposites on the great continuum of all life and creation. You are called to polarize ever toward the spiritual. Through your conscious efforts, give and you shall receive.

SEE IT'S A MATTER OF DEGREES

Poles apart, but sharing common ground.

Do you feel invisible at times and unable to influence events? Are you ready to let go of old thoughts and habitual behaviour?

The great Hermetic principle of Polarity reconciles aspects of our life and experiences that seem contradictory, shedding light on events and situations we may have found perplexing.

In interpersonal relationships, we've all heard the saying 'opposites attract'. But is there a deeper meaning here? The building blocks of life – atoms – are formed by the unity of positively and negatively charged particles. And the physical world provides many examples to illustrate this idea of opposites that complement and define each other – hot and cold, high and low, north and south, light and darkness.

This card invites you to explore your limitless potential. You have the ability to move – mind and being – along any continuum of polar opposites, from sadness to happiness, hate to love or fear to courage.

Use this key to unlock the door to the spiritual dimension. Matter and spirit lie at opposite ends of the same spectrum. It's just a matter of degrees. You are called to put this new understanding into practice – stop, breathe, allow yourself to be embraced by stillness. From here, everything is possible.

4 MOVE TOWARD SPIRIT

Shift, evolve, transform.

~

Do you find emotions inexplicable? Do you have many questions about spirituality?

The fourth Hermetic principle asks us to first observe the continuums of the physical world – hot/cold, wet/dry, high/low, dark/light, north/south.

By analogy, we see the connection to our mental life, how emotions we may have thought to be different in nature are simply a matter of degrees. For example, love and hate vibrate at opposite ends of the same spectrum. The same applies to fear and courage, sadness and happiness or negativity and positivity.

In the often-confusing area of spirituality, polarity is a trusted compass, a tool of navigation. In the bigger picture, we grasp that matter and spirit are opposite poles of a continuum, differentiated solely by level of vibration.

The fourth card in the suit of Polarity, 'Move toward spirit', calls you to lift your 'chemistry' in all that you feel, think and do. Free yourself of any identification with the lower aspects of your being, and consciously evolve along the continuum of being.

Gradually and steadily, bring about a shift from selfishness to selflessness, ignorance to enlightenment, *eros* (passionate love) to *agape* (love of mankind), directing your whole being towards the light.

VISUALIZE AND TRANSFORM

As light is the absence of dark, and vice versa, so is the unity of opposites in all worlds and planes.

Have your emotional highs been followed by lows? After success, have you ever felt a kind of backlash? Have you wondered about these contradictory emotions?

You're on the right path, it's just a question of direction. If you need to turn around, be kind to yourself as you gently pivot and re-orientate. Nothing is wasted. Everything you've seen and learned is needed now, as you step through the doorway of transformation.

Understanding Polarity simplifies and reconciles things that up to now may have seemed confusing. It is a unifying law, bringing together opposites on the different planes. These are all opposite ends of one and the same continuum. You can consciously move towards one or the other.

The fifth card in the suit of Polarity, 'Visualize and transform', is a call to your imagination, to 'see' and grasp the unity of opposites in nature, humanity and all of creation. Understand how this also applies to your mystical pilgrimage and the movement of spirit from fear to courage, darkness to illumination.

Through meditation and breath, come to stillness. From an inner place of love and kindness for your child spirit and divine potential, 'polarize' yourself along the continuum of being, toward your higher nature and soul potential.

6 THREAD THE SPECTRUM

Between extremes, the path to spirit beckons.

Have you ever been perplexed by feelings and emotional scenarios? Do you have many questions about spirituality?

The fourth great Hermetic principle illuminates our spiritual path in search of true purpose and destiny.

'Spectrum' is a word that crops up in everyday conversation, but here we apply it to different phenomena across the physical, mental and spiritual planes of existence.

The philosopher Plato declared, 'Serious things cannot be understood without laughable things; nor opposites without opposites.' The well-known yin and yang symbol is a visual reminder of the interconnectedness of opposites in all things, where yin represents the receptive and yang the active principle.

And in Chinese cosmology, the universe is conceived as the universal energy of 'qi' organizing countless units of yin and yang into the extraordinary diversity of our world.

The 'Thread the spectrum' card calls you to seek out the route that leads between extremes. You have the God-given ability to consciously influence where you sit on the great spectrum of all life and creation. This path of balance resolves opposition that may at first seem irreconcilable. This inner place, or state of mind, acts as a neutralizing force to give birth to new being, your divine provenance and potential to travel the worlds.

CONNECT, LIFT, ASCEND 7

Polarize your being – mind, body and soul – toward the light.

Have you ever felt isolated in a world of your own? Do you long for a deeper connection with others, and beyond?

The great Hermetic principle of Polarity expresses the creative tension of opposites present in all life and creation.

These opposing poles lie at either end of the countless continuums that form the universe, from the unity of positive and negative forces in infinitesimal atoms and molecules to the gravitational forces that hold stars, planets and moons in their orbital relationships.

In today's 21st-century world, we are all connected. This interchange at the speed of light is readily conceived in technological terms, via our use of online systems and devices. The ancient Hermetic wisdom, however, offers a profound glimpse of what connection means on all planes of existence, embracing mind, body and soul.

The seventh card in the suit of Polarity, 'Connect, lift, ascend', invites you to step through the portal that leads to new being, and a whole new understanding of who you are and what your true purpose is.

Use the creative tension of your efforts at 'conscious polarization'. Transform the raw material of your sensory experiences on the lower physical and mental planes, to open to experiences and knowledge in the spiritual dimension.

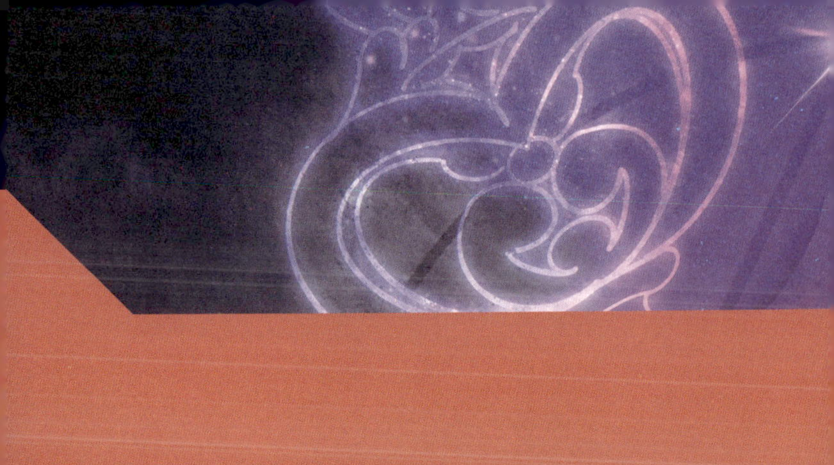

RHYTHM

V

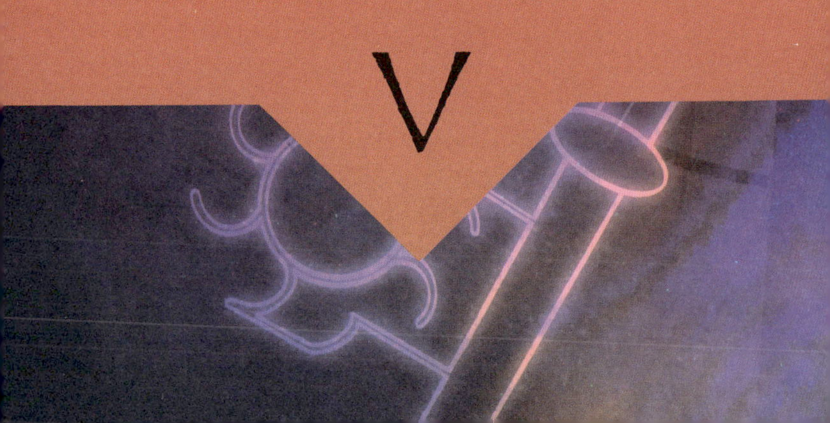

The pendulum swings
Ebb and flow,
the tides are fixed
Rise above the stream.

The fifth Hermetic principle of Rhythm highlights the cyclic nature of the world, around us and within. The swing of the Hermetic 'pendulum' explains many aspects of what we experience on the physical, mental and spiritual planes. The penny drops when we understand the saying, 'the pendulum swings' – a truth of great magnitude.

The pendulum is recognized in science as an instrument for measuring the effect of gravity. Gravitational force drives a pendulum's oscillation – its back-and-forth motion. The constancy of this swing allows pendulums to be used as a time-keeping element in clocks.

We are surrounded by the rhythms of nature, earthly and extra-terrestrial – sunrise and sunset, the ebb and flow of the tides, the four seasons of the calendar year, solstices and equinoxes, and the phases of the moon. Women and men are subject to regular hormonal patterns. Life and death, too, can be viewed as interdependent cycles that

govern all creation. One defines the other like swings of a pendulum.

From the biblical book, *Ecclesiastes*, the law of rhythm is given poetic expression: 'A time to give birth, and a time to die; a time to plant, and a time to uproot the plant. A time to kill, and a time to heal; a time to tear down, and a time to build. A time to weep, and a time to laugh.'

In the mental life of humankind, we see how emotions, moods, feelings and attitudes fluctuate from one to another, or between extremes. As in the physical world, all is in motion in one direction or another. It is an ever-changing melange – enthusiasm, depression, anxiety, euphoria, anger, humour, bravado, apprehension, phobia, indignation, gratitude, and so on.

However, the Hermetists recognize two levels of our mental life – unconscious and conscious. By practising what they call the Law of Neutralization, we rise above the swing of the pendulum and its unconscious, negative backlash. Nothing stops the pendulum. But, by an act of conscious will, we can observe the backswing and detach ourselves from it. We neutralize its impact.

As a result, instead of being carried this way and that, from one extreme to the other, we stand firm in the higher, positive aspect.

Applying the fifth principle to the mental plane, the Hermetists also refer to the Law of Compensation, which states that the energy or size of the swing in one direction determines the energy or size of the swing in the opposite direction. Similar to how the long upswing of a pendulum is counterbalanced by a long downswing, the more melancholic the person, the greater their capacity to experience joy or vice versa. A person able to experience only a little bit of pleasure is equally disposed to lesser pain.

But the Law of Compensation, relating to Rhythm, is perhaps best observed on the spiritual plane of people's lifetimes, including different lives. Even if you don't believe in reincarnation, you may be aware of individuals whose lives seem either cursed or charmed. From here, you may appreciate the argument that a person's current life may represent the counter swing, up or down, as a counterbalance to their previous lives. This aligns with the idea of the soul's journey or the 'wheel of karma' in the Buddhist and other traditions.

Again, the key learning here is that, with guided practice and discipline, we can develop our innate capacity to rise above our negative emotions or our suffering, which may seem unjustified or confusing at first. We may come to see it is karmic in nature.

It is important to grasp that a practical application of the Hermetic fifth principle does not promise the complete cessation of negative emotional or karmic experiences. Rather it is about learning to separate oneself from them and not be swept up in powerful currents.

Using the tools of mental transmutation, we ascend on the scale of being. It is a lifelong work.

UNDERSTAND THE PENDULUM

1

Everything arises and recedes, ebbs and flows, comes and goes in endless cycle.

Do you wonder about the cyclic nature of all life and the universe? Are you aware of repeated patterns that apply to your inner world, your thoughts and emotions?

The fifth great Hermetic principle of Rhythm expresses the law of the 'swing of the pendulum'. Think ebb and flow, action and reaction, up and down, motion and rest, the patterns and cycles of nature, the four seasons, the orbit of the earth, moon and planets, and the rhythms we are aware of on the inside – daily, monthly, hormonal, mental, psychological, generational, ancestral and karmic.

The first card in this suit calls you to cease all resistance. Its cyclic back-and-forth motion is a law governing everything, within and without. But when you tune in to major currents influencing the events of your life, and move in harmony with them, you learn to rise above the swing of the pendulum. You ascend the staircase that leads to illumination. You are called to harness your divine birthright. Take the conscious breath and bathe in inner stillness. From here, in tune with the law of rhythm – which applies on all realms, lower and higher – step through the portal of light that falls constant and eternal. Rise now and evolve toward the light.

2 CHANGE YOUR RHYTHM

To expand what you are seeing and feeling – stop, come to stillness, change your rhythm.

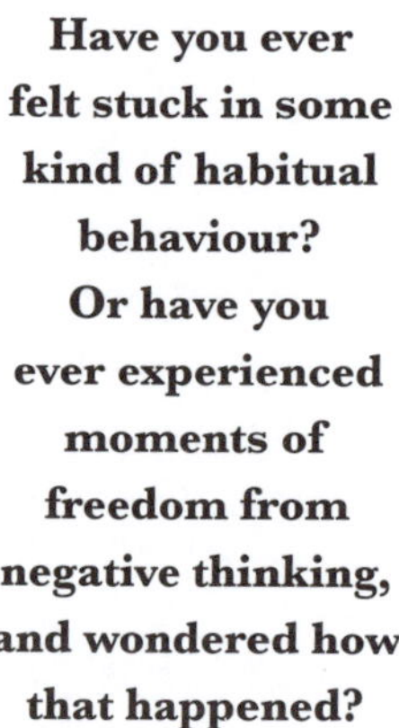

Have you ever felt stuck in some kind of habitual behaviour? Or have you ever experienced moments of freedom from negative thinking, and wondered how that happened?

There is a saying from the ancient practice of yoga: 'The mind is Lord of the senses, but the breath is Lord of the mind.' This offers a key to understanding rhythm, and how vital it is to our evolution as soul beings.

Our ordinary thoughts and mental states can be at the whim of our fears and hopes, stresses, imagination and the stream of images associated with those. By changing your rhythm through the conscious breath, you expand your consciousness.

Hold your attention on the inflow and outflow of breath. Take the breath from the crown (the top of your head), down through all seven chakras to the root centre (the sacrum at the base of your spine). After holding the 'breath-filled energy' there in stillness, release it back upwards on its reverse journey, upwards and back out through the crown chakra.

The second card in the Rhythm suit calls you to become aware of the connection between being and breath. You are a child of light. This is not just an idea. The breath is not only the practical foundation of human life, it is also the key to experiencing and realizing your soul potential.

HEAR THE RING OF TRUTH

Human life, the universe, and all creation express the patterns and energies of rhythm.

Have you ever noticed the power of sound and tempo to affect your moods and feelings? Do you find yourself attracted to particular types of music or songs? Is there a deeper message here?

Rhythm is intrinsic to all forms of language, and music is the purest language of all. Music can bring down or lift our emotions, stir our lower nature or inspire and evoke in us spirited and creative actions capable of transforming our world.

In a classical symphony or a contemporary pop song, we experience a blend of intensity and gentleness, where powerful sections give way to softer passages, or where melodies shift into counterpoint or an instrumental bridge.

The third card in the Rhythm suit, 'Hear the ring of truth', inspires you to listen to and feel music in a new way, in all its forms and styles, across all genres and cultures; to understand that music encapsulates the deepest understandings of human nature.

Just as it does in music and everything else, the pendulum swings in our inner world. You are called to listen with new understanding, to identify the level of being, life events and manifestations that different pieces of music attract.

Apply this understanding of rhythm to your own being, to enrich and unveil your soul purpose.

4 MASTER MOMENTUM

Evolve through understanding momentum on the physical, mental and spiritual planes.

Have you ever felt powerless as events progress in a certain direction? What does an understanding of momentum have to offer you?

As a powerful manifestation of rhythm, momentum can be observed in the sporting arena, in the way one team or opponent gains impetus during a competitive game. We also witness what you might understand as the 'return swing' of the pendulum, as the player or team with the initial ascendancy, inexplicably falters and the other lifts their performance and takes control.

Similarly, our emotions and thoughts can 'have a mind of their own' and carry us forward to conclusions we may find hard to avoid or refute. Momentum, once started, can be hard to resist or counterbalance; just as inertia, at the opposite end of the spectrum, can resist motion until it reaches a tipping point.

The fourth card in the Rhythm suit asks you to delve deep and call upon your inner resources – understanding, strength of will and purpose, the sense of 'something greater' or an intuition that there must be 'something more'. Know there is another way. The 'sceptre of power' lies within, ready when you are ready. Break your inertia in a situation you need to change and gain momentum on the path less travelled.

TO BEGIN, STOP

5

Stop, breathe, change your rhythm and direction, move towards the light.

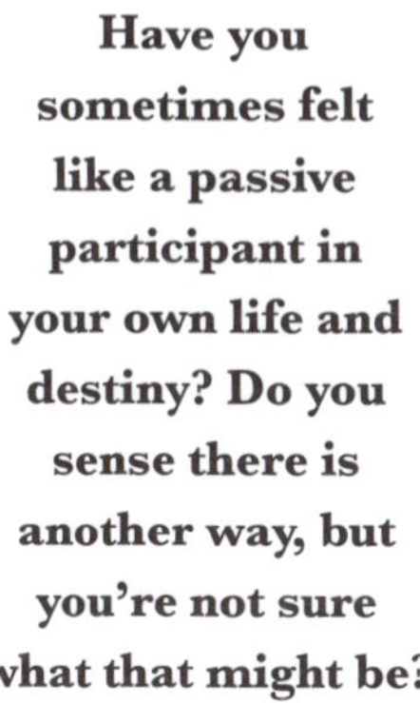

Have you sometimes felt like a passive participant in your own life and destiny? Do you sense there is another way, but you're not sure what that might be?

It is easy for us to feel swept along like flotsam by events or currents of opinion, ricocheting this way or that with the mass of humankind, like billiard balls racked up and set in motion by the thwack of a cue stick.

We can learn to 'neutralize' the effects of the 'swing of the pendulum' by 'lifting our chemistry' and vibration, to raise ourselves up and out of the unconsciousness that can rob human beings of their wondrous potential.

The fifth card in this suit, 'To begin, STOP', calls you to change your rhythm, whether you are caught in a rut or carried along in the momentum of strong thoughts and emotions. Ironically enough, a negative state of inertia requires you to STOP as much as the high-octane rush of action and reaction.

Learning to breathe consciously is an ancient practice conveyed to seekers and acolytes by the masters of all the great teachings. Breath is rhythm. To STOP, come to the conscious breath, lift your vibration and in stillness begin to walk the path of enlightenment.

6 WITHIN LAW, BECOME FREE

As we learn to harmonize with immutable laws, we earn the freedom to evolve toward the light.

Do you wish for change but you're unsure how to go about it? Do you feel stuck in a recurring pattern, even when you change your job, relationship or home?

Observing the 'swing of the pendulum' in the forces around and outside of us, we can begin to understand the inner disciplines we need to ascend the scale of being, moving from the physical to the mental plane and, higher again, to the spiritual.

The Hermetists extend this idea, asking us to observe how the Law of Compensation applies in everyday life – for example, how the things we gain are counterbalanced by the things we lose.

This Hermetic idea of compensation also applies to the 'chain of lives' or the soul's journey across multiple lifetimes. We see how an individual's suffering in one lifetime is compensated on the return 'swing of the pendulum' in a subsequent incarnation.

The sixth card in the suit of Rhythm, 'Within law, become free', calls you to understand the path to freedom. No one can change the laws that govern all of life and creation, but by learning to rise above the pendulum as it swings on different planes of being, you progress along the path of soul growth that leads ever onward and upward.

TAKE THE HIGH ROAD 7

On the high road, rise above the swing of the pendulum on all levels and planes.

Do you wish for change but you're unsure how to go about it? Do you feel stuck in a recurring pattern of highs and lows, affecting key aspects of your life such as your job, relationship or home?

Throughout history, great civilizations have risen and fallen. Similarly, social movements arise and subside, leaders in science, politics, religion and spirituality come and go, leaving legacies of progress or darkness.

Concerning rhythm in the realm of human mental activity, the Hermetic masters speak of the Law of Neutralization. Here, the swing of the pendulum is evident in the fluctuating moods, feelings and thoughts that accompany and affect our day-to-day living. However, by consciously resisting the pull in one direction, then the other, we can develop a muscle that, over time, stabilizes our emotional life.

The seventh card in the suit of Rhythm, 'Take the high road', calls you to lift your vibration and consciousness to a higher plane. The rhythm of the pendulum is always in force. However, by raising your mental vibration from the lower level (unconsciousness) to the higher (consciousness), you have the potential to rise above the swing of the pendulum on the unconscious plane and escape its backlash.

CAUSE AND EFFECT

VI

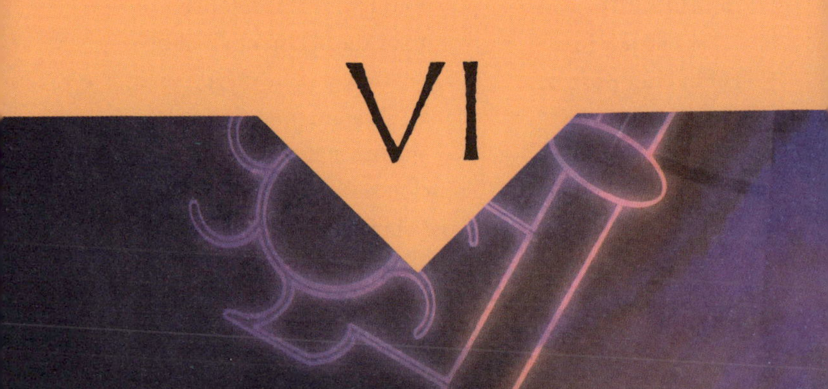

Nothing falls by chance
Just forest forces unknown
Be cause, not effect.

The sixth great principle of the Hermetic system, 'Cause and Effect', declares that everything happens for a reason. Nothing is left to chance. The adage 'You make your own luck' is more to

the point, suggesting that human beings have the potential to consciously influence life events.

In a universe governed by laws, the Hermetists say that what we commonly call 'chance' refers to events with causes we don't know or understand. For anything that happens, there must be preceding events, actions or manifestations of one kind or another. For example, we may speak of an unexpected 'windfall', a mishap or a personal experience that was unlucky or fortuitous. Although such events may be unpredictable, the law of cause and effect still applies.

A mighty tree falls in the forest. No human may have known about or anticipated this sudden incident, but that does not make it a random or chance occurrence. Scientific scrutiny would likely reveal the toll over many years of such causative factors as erosion of the soil, the impact of strong winds, disintegration of its trunk and root system during prolonged periods of drought, and, at last, the collapse of a major branch, causing an imbalance that finally toppled the tree to the ground.

We say someone who wins the lottery has been blessed by 'Lady Luck', but the cause of their success is clear: they submitted a sequence of numbers matching those that were electronically drawn.

Similarly, on the mental plane, for every feeling, thought or emotion, there is a cause, and causes are, in turn, the effect of preceding feelings, emotions and thoughts. But this is not to say the flow of associations of the inner life of humankind can never be more than reactive and mechanical, like an internal snooker game, with balls colliding and moving off in all directions. The Hermetic teaching is that the principle of Cause and Effect is always in operation. The main thing is to see, experience, and understand its workings on different planes.

As part of the process of self-mastery, we have the ability to learn to work with the sixth principle more and more consciously. Once we understand the rules of the game, we learn to rise above material existence and not just be swept this way and that by so-called 'chance' events and circumstances, including fluctuating moods, feelings and emotions that so often dominate life.

The Hermetists call us to realize our potential to be much more than pawns moved by external forces on life's chequerboard. With growing understanding, we transition from the physical to the mental, and on to the spiritual plane. As we learn to be 'rulers' on the lower planes so, in turn, we become 'servants' on the higher planes. The challenge is to develop our divine potential to become a 'cause' instead of an 'effect'.

ALLOW FOR CAUSE

1

For everything that happens there is a cause.

Have you ever felt your life to be jinxed? Do you often see yourself as 'out of luck' or regard some people as living 'charmed' lives?

The sixth great Hermetic axiom of Cause and Effect says there is no such thing as chance or luck. There is a cause for everything that happens in our world and the universe.

Everyday events are commonly described as 'random' or 'accidental'. However, the Hermetists tell us that 'chance' is simply a label we use when we don't know the actual causes. For example, when we toss a coin, 'heads' is the result of holding the coin in a certain way and flicking it upwards at a certain angle and velocity. If we could lift the same coin in precisely the same way again and perform an identical sequence of muscular actions a second time, heads would come up again. However, it is impossible to repeatedly toss the same coin in exactly the same way.

The first card in the suit of Cause and Effect, 'Allow for cause', calls on you to reframe your purpose and higher destiny. You are a player in your own life. What you do and what you achieve in this lifetime is not the result of blind forces at play. Your level of evolution and being determines what you attract, unconsciously or consciously.

2 BECOME A MOVER

By raising our level of consciousness, we are able to influence events on higher levels and planes.

~

Do you feel unable to attract the life you seek, or pushed this way and that by random events? Do you believe you have no control in your life?

The sixth great Hermetic principle of Cause and Effect states that 'every cause has its effect; every effect has its cause' and what we call 'chance' is simply a name for events where the causes are unknown to us.

On the physical level, weather events like storms, drought or tsunamis are the effects of preceding meteorological conditions. In the mental dimension, emotions, thoughts and opinions spark each other in an endless chain of cause and effect. On the spiritual plane, experiences on one level may prepare the way for experiences of a higher level.

The 'Become a mover' card calls you to learn the ways of mental alchemy and self-mastery and become more than just a link in an unconscious chain of cause and effect.

By understanding and applying the principle of causation, you lift your chemistry and consciousness above the mechanical laws of a particular plane and move higher on the scale of being. You have the divine potential to be far more than just a pawn in the game of life and creation. Become a 'cause', not just an 'effect'. Lift your level of being and move towards the light.

WILL TO BE FREE

We may think we have little influence over events that form the narrative of our lives. However, one of the great provocations of 'mental transmutation' is that we can consciously move or 'polarize' ourselves toward the positive end of the continuums that define our lives.

The Hermetists reframe the traditional 'free will' versus 'determinism' debate telling us that neither is right or wrong; that both are 'half-truths' representing opposite poles of a sliding scale. As we become more conscious, we move away from 'unconsciousness' toward 'free will' or vice versa.

Consciousness opens the door to free will and experience of higher dimensions.

~

Are you just going through the motions? Has your life felt like a bit of a sleepwalk at times? Are you ready to explore another way?

The third card in this suit inspires you to embark on a journey of liberation. Understand that every event, interaction or manifestation in the physical, mental, and spiritual dimension occurs as a direct result of preceding events. 'Chance' is just a label for causes we can't see or identify.

Through the lens of the principle of cause and effect, you are called to understand that everything you think, feel and do has history, impact, and purpose. See the world in a whole new light of consciousness. Seize the day – *carpe diem*!

4 KNOW IT'S 'MEANT TO BE'

Allow for the guidance of higher intelligence.

Are you open to higher dimensions? In times of crisis, have you ever found yourself reaching out to angelic beings? Do you wish to know more about your higher purpose?

Is life a series of unforeseen, random events or is there always a higher purpose at work? The sixth great Hermetic principle of Cause and Effect tells us that everything happens according to the laws that apply across the physical, mental and spiritual planes. Even if we cannot identify the reasons behind events, they are still subject to universal law.

We say, 'It was meant to be' or just as often, 'It wasn't meant to be'. Curiously, this acknowledges there must be a cause, even if we don't know what that is. You might win the lottery; you meet your soulmate unexpectedly; or you get a gut feeling not to board a train that later derails. It appears the more significant these events are, the more willing we are to acknowledge a higher intelligence and not just put it all down to chance.

This card urges you to honour a higher dimension, to grasp the truth that you have a higher purpose. With your every belief, transform the cause and effect that creates your future. It is a two-way process: give and you will receive. Focus your intent, lift your vibration, breathe consciously, and open your heart to your divine destiny.

RELEASE YOUR SOUL

Believe you are a soul being, take the path of transformation.

~

Do you believe in the world of soul, or that you have a soul? Have you ever sensed there is a spiritual dimension to your life, or that your soul has a higher purpose?

Up to now, you may have viewed the world as a haphazard affair, where the fate of human beings is also unpredictable. Interestingly though, particularly in competitive sport, there is also a saying, 'you make your own luck'.

The sixth great Hermetic principle tells us there is a cause for everything that happens in our world and the universe. We only speak of 'luck' when the causes are simply unknown to us.

The fifth card in the suit of Cause and Effect, 'Release your soul', inspires you to reframe your life, purpose, and higher destiny. Not as a matter of faith or hope, but because you can. You have the power to do this. You stand at the brink of new direction, life and being.

Believe and know you are a player in your own life; that what you do and what you achieve in this lifetime is not the result of blind forces at play, but of what you attract, unconsciously or consciously. You can be inactive or reactive – or *proactive*. You are called to activate your true destiny. You have the innate ability to realize your divine potential, to step through this magical portal of light and set your soul free, in this life and the next.

6 TREK THE HOLY

When your ears are ready to hear, the whisper of truth comes in close.

~

Are you ready for a new knowledge and way of living? Do you feel a need for fresh understanding of your life and purpose?

The sixth great Hermetic principle of Cause and Effect confirms the truth of the saying, 'everything happens for a reason'. As always, however, the Hermetists take it a step further, with the idea that not only is there no such thing as 'chance' but, according to esoteric law, for every cause and effect, there is a higher purpose.

There is much we do not know about ourselves and the place of humankind within the cosmos. The Hermetic principles work together as a whole. The second axiom of Correspondence, or 'As above, so below', helps us grasp the higher meaning of the principle of Cause and Effect, by asking us to consider the existence of a 'Prime mover' in the universe – the mind of THE ALL. You too can become a 'mover' – a creator in your own right.

This card calls us to embark on a journey into the unknown, to lift our vibration and the 'chemistry' of our being. In this state of readiness, the old Hermetic truth applies, 'When the ears of the student are ready to hear, then cometh the lips to fill them with wisdom.' Know it is your birthright – your potential to transform from passive to an active link in a chain of cause and effect. Give birth to your true self.

BE SERVANT AND MASTER

7

Serve your apprenticeship on every level of being within the physical, mental and spiritual planes.

Are you prepared to learn the timeless ways of the ancients? Do you understand that giving with all your heart and soul, will attract gifts of the spirit?

The Hermetic principle of Cause and Effect applies on all levels and subdivisions of the great physical, mental and spiritual planes. Everything that happens is the result of that which preceded it, and every 'effect', in turn, is a necessary condition of all that follows. In all of life and creation, nothing is left to chance.

We 'serve our apprenticeship' at every stage of soul development. Moving ever upward, we ascend to the next level, again to embrace the role of 'servant', preparing, when we are ready, to rise further on the scale of being.

The seventh card in this suit reminds you there are no shortcuts on your soul journey. Knowledge may be power, but humility enriches understanding. Vulnerability is the fertile soil from which emerges strength of a higher order.

Everything is relative in all of life, creation and the universe. In the timeless wisdom of mental alchemy, you are both cause and effect. To achieve self-mastery, embrace servitude with all your heart. Understand that the path to self-mastery opens the portal of soul ascension.

GENDER

VII

Hills and stars they spin
Masculine and feminine
Their tension's the thing.

The seventh and final great Hermetic principle, Gender, is more about energy of mind than one's physical attribution or sexual identification. It sheds fresh light on the meaning of male/female or masculine/feminine.

The Hermetic understanding of gender is that of 'creating, producing, generating' on every level of phenomena, across the three great planes: physical, mental and spiritual. The word 'gender' derives from the Latin noun *genus*, meaning 'family' or 'birth', which is related to the verb *generare*, which means to 'beget', 'procreate' or 'produce'.

To begin, there can be no better illustrative example than the very building blocks of matter, atoms. Here we see positively charged 'protons' attracting negatively charged 'electrons', which orbit each nucleus, like nanoscopic moons around the most minuscule of planets.

Atoms – for example, carbon, nitrogen, oxygen and so on, as listed in the table of elements – are held together energetically by the attraction between negative electrons and positively charged protons. These combine with other atoms or elements to form molecules of matter. Countless configurations form the world around us – mountains, seas, planets and stars, and living organisms, such as animals, plants and humans.

For the Hermetists, all life and creation is the result of the principle of gender in action. Negative is designated 'feminine', and 'masculine' is positive. But not in the everyday sense of a negative or positive thought, attitude or opinion. Rather, the feminine aspect is the wellspring of creativity, and the masculine is the active, initiating force.

On the physical plane, the birth of offspring in different species is easy to understand as the organic result of the sexual union between male and female. Both are needed for something new to emerge from the interaction. On the higher, non-physical planes, a similar relationship holds between the feminine and the masculine, but this is purely energetic in nature. It takes place within the one person or between different individuals.

The principle of Gender describes a 'duality of mind', between 'I' and 'me'. For most of us, the 'me' is the aspect of self we are almost solely identified with. In fact, we often mistake 'me' – referring to our bodies or physical identities and sensations, our emotional makeup, moods, likes, dislikes, tastes and preferences – for 'I' which is underdeveloped, if it exists at all.

To explain this further, the Hermetists say the masculine 'I' is quite separate to the feminine 'me'. The

latter is akin to a 'mental womb', the seat of imagination, creative thought and expression. The key to grasping the relationship between the two, is to understand the 'I' as a product of will – more about the nature of 'being' – as distinct from 'me' which is about 'becoming'.

Both are needed for evolution, for new life and creation. Without the feminine, the masculine acts in a void, like an artist without instrument or medium. Conversely, without the masculine impulse, the feminine lacks direction, lost in a spin of potentiality and possibilities, unable to act.

By way of example, we may observe in ourselves or others, the ability to act and produce original results in some field or endeavour, or a tendency to generate ideas only, without bringing any of those ideas to fruition. Both situations can be understood with reference to the Hermetic principle of gender.

This principle also sheds light on 'psychic' phenomena', such as the power of suggestion, hypnotism, telepathy, and the like, including the ability of stage or movie actors to stir the feelings and emotions of their audience. Here we see individuals providing the masculine or initiating impulse, which conveys an idea or thought to their subject, who receives this suggestion in a feminine or receptive state.

Powerful or charismatic leaders are scattered throughout history, able to influence the thinking and emotions of legions of followers, for good or bad. The fact that they are such memorable figures may suggest the masculine principle lies mostly dormant within and among us, whether you are male or female. When it emerges in rare individuals in politics, science or the arts in any society or time in history, its legacy can be lasting and never to be forgotten.

The Hermetic principle of Gender is a call, in the words of the Delphic Oracle, to truly 'know thyself', activating the inner relationship between 'I' and 'me' and the possibility of giving birth to your true self, one capable of realizing its divine potential and birthright.

BALANCE MASCULINE AND FEMININE

The inner interplay of gender is the source of your soul realization.

Are you aware of your inner masculine and the feminine aspects? Are you ready to unlock your creative potential?

Every human being has a mother and father. The biological union of the masculine and feminine is miraculous in its own right. However, the seventh great Hermetic principle of Gender applies across all levels of existence – physically, mentally and spiritually.

The creative interplay of the masculine and feminine principles applies at the nanoscopic level of fundamental particles, all the way up to the manifestation of suns, planets and moons in our universe. It encompasses a vast continuum of being, with every manifestation of matter and energy differentiated as always by vibratory degree.

The first card in the suit of Gender, 'Balance masculine and feminine', calls you to expand your understanding of this eternal truth and its application to your inner world; to grasp and turn this key of mental alchemy, sparking your inner creative force and focus to give birth to your sacred, higher self.

New life and new being are yours to make a reality in this lifetime. Both the masculine and feminine principles are latent within you. You have the capacity to awaken them in creative union, tension and harmony and rise upward on the scale of being to make your higher purpose a reality.

2 IGNITE THE CREATIVE

The inner interplay of gender is the source of your true creativity.

~

Are you aware of your inner masculine and the feminine aspects? Are you ready to unlock your creative potential?

The physical or biological 'male/ female' distinction, is just the beginning of grasping the Hermetic conception of gender. As we've seen, the word derives from the Latin *genus* meaning 'birth' or 'family' and the French *genre* meaning 'of a kind'.

The building blocks of all life and creation – atoms – are expressions of the masculine and feminine principle, held together by the attraction between negative 'electrons' and positive 'protons'. The dynamic tension of this relationship is the basis of the Hermetic concept of gender as it applies on other levels and planes of existence.

The second card in the suit of Gender, 'Ignite the creative', calls you to embark on an esoteric journey of discovery. Everything you need is already given. You just need to begin the process. By exploring the creative interplay of masculine and feminine in all of life, nature and the interconnectedness of human beings, understand how this also applies to your inner life, your soul quest and realization of your divine potential.

ATTRACT MATESHIP OF SOUL

On all levels of being, the interplay of masculine and feminine sparks soul connection.

~

Do you seek soul connection in a relationship? Have you been looking for someone else to make you whole?

The seventh great Hermetic principle of Gender lifts our modern-day notions about gender identity to a higher power, from the physical and mental planes, to the spiritual.

We all have the masculine and feminine principles within – the active 'I' and the receptive 'me'. However, this often plays out between two people in the ordinary world – in both male-female and same-sex partnerships – with little understanding of what is happening. One tends to dominate the other rather than allowing for each individual's innate capacity to realize their creative potential.

The third card in the suit of Gender, 'Attract mateship of soul', calls you to separate from your emotions, moods, associative thoughts, likes and dislikes and counterbalance these with a simple stillness of being. Come in touch with the masculine and feminine within your being.

In this way, prepare to attract a relationship with another human being that mirrors this creative complementarity. Now, with your combined vibration becoming ever higher and finer, step forward on your soul journey.

4 SEPARATE 'I' FROM 'ME'

The interplay of the masculine 'I' and the feminine 'me' is the hub of creativity.

Do you struggle to put your creative ideas into action? Have you ever wondered why people may have great difficulty in finishing projects and initiatives?

The Hermetic principle of Gender makes a distinction between 'I' and 'me' – respectively, the masculine and feminine principles. At first, this may seem counterintuitive. We observe that many people focus their attention and mental energy on their bodily nature and its appetites, as if this is where their core sense of self resides.

For the Hermetists, 'me' includes our daily stream of feelings, actions and reactions, emotions, tastes and aversions, likes, dislikes, habits, peculiarities and so on. Taken as a whole, these form the 'I am' of an average individual. But this is only half the story.

In mental alchemy, the 'me' aspect of mental gender is our seat of creativity, including ideas and psychic intuitions. The 'I' aspect is characterized as 'initiating force', a manifestation of 'will' able to ignite and give direction to the feminine, intuitive side of our nature. Together, they enable action and results.

This card calls you to examine your inner world honestly and courageously. What do you need to let go of, and what do you need to develop? It is important to begin.

UNIFY OPPOSITES

Gender is expressed in the unity of opposites – active/ passive, negative/ positive, masculine/ feminine.

~

When you find the time to act, have you ever lost motivation or been unable to act? Do your best ideas come at inconvenient times, when you're doing something else?

The male/female duality is just one physical expression of the vast sphere of application of this seventh great Hermetic principle.

The creative tension between the masculine and the feminine underlies everything manifest in life, nature and the universe. In the Hermetic system, gender relates to much more than sexuality – it is about the unity of opposite forces: active/passive, action/reaction, negative/positive.

The fifth card in the suit of Gender, 'Unify opposites' asks you grasp the energetic axis of all life and creation, of every event and form of matter, animate or inanimate. Both the impulse of the masculine and the receptivity of the feminine are latent within you, awaiting the focus of your will and attention to be activated. Whatever you can imagine can become your reality.

To truly act, initiate or make your ideas a reality, bring your inner masculine and feminine together as one. Now become a creator in your own right.

6 BECOME YOUR TRUE SELF

Your level of being attracts your life.

~

Have you ever asked yourself who you are? Do you seek a deeper sense of self? Have you wondered about your true purpose and destiny?

The seventh great Hermetic principle of Gender offers a key to many mysterious phenomena across all the planes of being – physical, mental and spiritual. These include the invisible realms of light, heat, electricity, magnetism, attraction and repulsion – and in relation to the mental dimension, through psychic phenomena such as telepathy, thought transference, mental influence, suggestion or hypnotism. Here we see the active force of the masculine, galvanizing the receptive, boundless creativity of the feminine aspect.

Without the 'being' of an individual, unique 'I', a person's 'me' aspect – described as feminine and receptive – may be vulnerable to whatever suggestion is received from an external source; in this case an individual in whom a strong sense of 'I' has been crystallized.

This card inspires you to understand what focus, will and attention can achieve in respect to the duality of masculine and feminine forces of the true 'I am'. With courage and honesty, face and do not shirk responsibility from what you see is missing. Take action to restore the creative interplay of 'I' and 'me' and become who you are truly meant to be – a soul being.

KNOW IT'S ALL ABOUT ENERGY

Life, creation and the universe – it's all about energy.

Have you ever felt suddenly tired or energized in different company? Would you like to understand more about energy?

In Hermetic wisdom, Gender is about pure energy. At the atomic level of the physical world, masculine ('positive') protons and feminine ('negative') electrons combine to form the building blocks of the universe. This energetic relationship also applies on the mental and spiritual planes.

The seventh card in the suit of Gender asks you to come in touch with the masculine ('I') and feminine ('me') energies within yourself. Both are needed for the realization of any idea or creative project, or on the spiritual level, to develop your soul potential.

From male/female on the biological or physical level, move to an understanding of what 'masculine/ feminine' means on the mental and spiritual planes. Bringing the two into balance supports your journey toward higher consciousness.

Allow yourself to be illumined by the spiritual energetic archetype expressed in Chinese cosmology as yin and yang, the receptive and active principles, the creative tension and union of opposites from which emerges all life, creation and the universe. You stand at the top of a staircase, a dazzling portal has opened. It is waiting for you. No turning back now, as you step forward to bathe in the light of illumination, new life and being.

ABOUT THE AUTHOR

For over 25 years, Steve has been a member of a meditation-based esoteric school in Sydney, practicing the conscious breath and stillness as the foundation of fulfilling one's soul potential. At the age of 18, he had a sudden awakening, an experience he describes as 'being struck by, and filled with light'. Since that moment, he has pursued the meaning of his true destiny and how to meld his creative gifts into day-to-day life.

From the age of nine, his heart has always answered the call of poetry and art, to make music with words and imagery. To be able to compose in this way, not in isolation but creative interplay with wife, Emma Wertheim, is a gift and a shared joy.

Steve's lifelong passion for drawing and painting has accelerated in recent years. His prolific output is in evidence online at Bluethumb – Home of Australian artists (bluethumb.com.au). Again, in collaboration with Emma, his artwork also appears in a retail line of greeting cards published in 2023 by Watermark Enterprises.

His book of social commentary, 'A Plate of Eggs' was published in 2011 by Zeus and he has been shortlisted, commended or highly commended for several Australian poetry prizes including the Blake Prize for Poetry (2017), the Australian Catholic University Prize for Poetry (2019, 2021, 2023, 2024) and the Lambing Flat (Federation of Australian Writers) Poetry Prize (2019, 2024).

Steve holds degrees in philosophy and psychology from the University of Sydney. He is also qualified with diplomas in Graphic Design and Creative Communications.

ACKNOWLEDGEMENTS

To Emma, my soulmate in spirit, life and love of cats – I thank you for your gift of seeing where I am heading or need to go in all things creative.

My heartfelt gratitude also goes to Tania Ahsan and all the team at Arcturus Publishing for their amazing support of this project.

CARD INDEX

I. THE ALL is Mind

II. Correspondence

III. Vibration

IV. Polarity

V. Rhythm

VI. Cause and Effect

VII. Gender